T5-CQC-293

# WOMEN
## of my
# OTHER
# WORLDS

# WOMEN
## of my
# OTHER
# WORLDS

*Olivia Casberg*

OLIVE PRESS PUBLICATIONS
P.O. BOX 99
LOS OLIVOS, CALIFORNIA 93441

**Library of Congress Cataloging in Publication Data**

Casberg, Olivia, 1910–
    Women of my other worlds.

    1. Women—India—Biography—Anecdotes, facetiae, satire,
etc. 2. Women—China—Biography—Anecdotes, facetiae, satire,
etc. 3. Women—Anecdotes, facetiae, satire, etc. 4. Casberg,
Olivia, 1910–        I. Title.
CT3720.C37  1985          920.72'0954          84-27221
ISBN 0-933380-30-5

**Olivia Casberg**

955 Elk Grove Lane
(805) 688-5036          Solvang, California 93463

*What an oasis you gave us during
Our days together in India !*

*Olivia*

Also by Olivia Casberg

# MISSION THROUGH A WOMAN'S EYES

# Table of Contents

"What is bettre than wisdom? -- *Woman.*

And what is bettre than a good woman?
-- *Nothing.*"

— *Chaucer*

## Lines for Soong Ching Ling

Three years without you
Who adorned our century
With beauty, courage, constancy.
A beacon in its adversities,
A glad light in its triumphs.

Shanghai girl,
Warm, sparkling, serene,
How wondrously you grew.

Schooled abroad, lifelong for China
Reared in comfort, choosing struggle
Staunch backer of frontline fighters,
Sharer of the underground's perils,
Your all for the people, the revolution,
        the children, the future
Under the dawning star.

Modest, how high you stood,
Low-voiced, yet heard worldwide.
Gentle, yet iron strong,
Graceful, by no storms bent.

More imperishable than your statue's marble
Your spirit's unquenchable fire,
Pure, changeless, fearless, tireless,
igniting new hearts
to adorn new centuries.

Israel Epstein
Shanghai Jan. 27, 1984
(Written following the unveiling of her statue)
My deep appreciation to Israel Epstein and to the Editorial Staff of
China Reconstructs for the use of the picture of Soong Ching Ling's
statue, and the poem by Israel Epstein.

# The
# Great Lady of China
# —Madam Sun Yat-sen

Five thousand Chinese Communists watched us as we were ushered to our seats in the Sun Yat-sen Hall, a memorial built to honor the husband of the lady I was to interview later. Four seats had been left empty for our interpreters, my husband and me. I was just plain scared; for it was only a few weeks after Nixon had visited the People's Republic of China. Twenty-five years of propaganda against Americans had been given their youth.

As soon as we were seated, the music began. Two-and-a-half hours later, an appreciative applause ended the perfect concert. We got up to leave and immediately another - and greater applause - broke out. We started back to our seats for the expected encore, but our interpreters stopped us, "No, our audience is applauding for *you*."

"What do we do?"

"Just clap back at them, and they will be happy."

An invitation to dinner had awaited our arrival in Peking. Madam Sun broke custom by giving us dinner in her home. For 40 years I had heard of her. Dr. Casberg had known her well during his war years in China. When he left in 1944 he had asked her, "What will you do in a China soon to be torn by civil war?" She had answered with another question, as is the oriental custom, "Dr. Casberg, do you have children? When they are in trouble, do you leave them? I shall remain in China no matter what happens and serve my people."

Two beautiful girls helped her to her chair at the head of the table. "Please meet my goddaughters. One is in the Army and soon to be a student at Stanford. The other belongs to the Navy and is a ballet dancer."

Her 85 years didn't show. Her black hair and lack of wrinkles made her look 20 years younger. Her alert mind was quick to respond to my question as to how she had spent the Mao years. "For 40 years I have given my life to the children of China. You can see they are the healthiest, the most uninhibited, yet well-disciplined youth in the world."

"Dr. and I surely agree, for we have visited on the farms, in the Communes and in the cities; we have studied their medical care with the barefoot doctors and noted their nutrition, and what you say is true."

"Do you hear from your sister, Madam Chiang Kai-shek?"

"O yes, she lives in New York. It seems she is dying of cancer and is reticent to be seen in public, so she goes about in disguise."

"And what about your sister, Madam Kung, who married the banker?"

"I read," she mused, "that she has passed on."

"Have you ever regretted staying in China?"

"No, I have been busy. I have seen my people delivered from famine, disease, drug addiction and banditry. 'Forget self, live for others' is a motto displayed on our streets, and my people are learning."

I thought as I left that evening that Madam Sun must find real inner peace, having made her decision to remain with her people, who today honor her as they honor her husband, the Father of the Republic, a man respected by all factions of China -- the late President Sun Yat-sen.

What a legacy she has left!

# My
# Hindu Friend

---

It was midnight in Agra. Aishi and I stood in bright moonlight, transfixed by the sight before us. One of the Wonders of the World, The Taj Mahal, with its glittering jewels, shimmered in the full moon of India. Our spirits blended. She of the Hindu faith and I of Christian talked of our gods and prayer. She shared with me how her god had worked miracles in her life.

Aishi and I walked the streets of Delhi together many times. We searched out shops in Old Delhi where we found wedding saris -- saris loaded with gold embroidery. "This is far too expensive," I said as the old shopkeeper, sitting cross-legged in front of me, threw those five yards across my lap. "But," I mused, "this may be my last trip to India."

And so I walked out of the shop with something special, something I could wear in any gathering of distinguished Indians and feel their approval, especially Aishi's. They love to see us wear their costume when it's draped authentically. Acceptance in a foreign country is so important if one hopes to be effective.

Aishi and her husband, Pran, visited the U.S. some years later, saw Disneyland and shared our home for a time. I began to open my mind to the beliefs of others, walls of prejudice came down, and I listened. I learned to admire her, to be tolerant of her ideas, and love her for what she was -- a Hindu Lady.

# *Dhoma,*
# *the Tibetan Vendor*

---

The temperature of one hundred twenty degrees warned us of impending summer discomfort. Mothers of students in an American school in the Himalayas began packing for six or eight weeks of vacation from the scorched plains. Our children took their leave from school in the winter, so as to be with parents in the cool season on the plains. Their studies then continued on through June and July - 7,000 feet above sea level. So - to the hills, Mom. Dad will join the family when his work permits.

When foreign families gather in these high altitude areas, *always*, vendors -- crowds of vendors -- follow: vegetable wallas, buffalo milk men, and coke-for-cooking carriers. Here gather the Chinese "Johns" with their huge bundles of merchandise on bicycles.

This year, among them was a Tibetan

woman. Dhoma had fled Tibet with the Dalai Lama. She joined a straggling group of refugees who crossed the border into North India.

Dhoma knew English and very soon we became friends. She would open her bags of curios and spread them all over the front room floor: precious stones, Tibetan horns, antique trays and kettles of various sizes and shapes. The metal work was done in silver and copper. In fact, the use of these two metals has become a trademark of Tibetan crafts.

One day I said, "Dhoma, won't you have tea with me?"

"Oh, I mustn't, Memsahib, we are from two different worlds!" But we ended up drinking tea together.

"Dhoma, have you children?"

"No," she dropped her head modestly, "but I am expecting a child soon." She was past 40, and I felt she needed professional care, but she assured me that she could manage.


Five years later I returned to India and we found Dhoma in New Delhi among her Tibetan friends selling their goods from tiny stalls on the sidewalks. She had her little boy!

# Dr. Ida

I was taken into her parlor. The great lady of medicine, Dr. Ida Scudder, was past 80, sitting in her wheel chair, wrapped in a warm lap robe. Someone had told her of my years in sacred music. "Olivia, would you sing my favorite hymn?"

I looked about for an instrument and saw a tired old piano. I knew it would be out of tune. All pianos in the Orient are out of tune. How well I recall listening to a tape of Albert Schweitzer playing on his Lamberene piano. I couldn't believe the great musician tolerated those blue notes. But that's how it is over there. I sat down and with a few opening chords began her favorite song. She cried a little.

Dr. Ida opened a hospital in South India which has become a monument of Christian concern for the sick of a great continent. One of their most

10

famous contributions is the Rehabilitation Center for lepers.

A most unusual woman, -- she! The doctor who followed her as Director of Vellore remarked one day to me: "She has never told me how to manage my new duties -- never once interfered with my decisions."

Perhaps because I pleased Dr. Ida that day, she asked if I would enjoy a ride in the country with her. We drove through rice fields and tropical forests to her favorite mountain. She said, "You know what I call that mountain? I call him Moses. I talk to Moses often. He hears my complaints, my joys, my problems in the hospital, and my hopes for the future."

Do *you* have a mountain to talk to? I have one now. It is called Mt. Condor. And I built a home where a window frames my mountain.

# The Madonna

## on the Roof

---

It was the morning of Independence Day in Delhi. The day was clear and cold. I awakened in my warm hotel room and began dressing for breakfast. My attention was captured by a scene across the busy street on the rooftop of a dingy old structure.

There, to my amazement, sat a mother with two small children without shelter of any kind. They were clothed as many children are in India, with only a shirt. I wondered if that was the way they control dirty pants or having little cloth -- settle for the warmer shirt instead of pants? There was no sign of a daddy. Perhaps he was off on a coolie job somewhere. No furniture was evident except for a small charcoal mud stove in one dark corner. As I pondered my own meal I wondered what she might be preparing for the one child whom she no longer put to her breast. Then, I noticed she was rolling out a piece of dough into a chapatti, something like a tortilla. This, with some pepper sauce, would be the only food the little two-year-old would have until evening. No milk. No fruit. No eggs. No wonder there are so many deaths for the child just weaned. As I stood there at my window I remembered looking down long aisles of a supermarket with its hundreds of brightly decorated cans -- carefully balanced meat and fish delights guaranteed to have all the vitamins needed to keep them healthy and their fur thick and shiny. "Oh God," I said to myself audibly, "Dogs eat better in America than these babies!" Parading elephants, camels and bands of musicans passed by us that day. I, in my warm hotel room; the little mother on the roof across the way.

How would you feel!

# The

# Barefoot Doctor

She is neither barefoot, nor is she a doctor.

Barefoot doctors are divided about evenly between boys and girls. She is very young, yet she serves in a fascinating way in China. It is estimated that there is about one barefoot doctor to every one hundred persons.

Our barefoot doctor is given first-aid training for three months initially. She then goes to work in her own community, giving shots, delivering babes, and teaching preventive medicine. She carries a medical kit with simple medicines and acupuncture needles and usually rides a bicycle from place to place. She has a small office and radio connection with the Commune Hospital and when she has a case too difficult for her to manage, she gets in touch with the hospital and arranges for transportation for the patient.

Each year she adds to her medical knowledge

by taking more training, either in a hospital environment or from doctors who travel about the countryside giving advanced study to the barefoot doctors.

One preventive medicine law she has managed to get across well: All drinking water must be boiled. There must be a billion thermoses in China -- all filled each morning with boiling water. But what a miracle it has worked! That, plus a pretty well-balanced diet and without a lot of sweets, has made the healthiest population we saw anywhere in the Orient.

By our standards, the barefoot doctor is no more than an Army first-aid corpsman, but it is terribly important to have that first contact for the sick.

# The

# Coolie Woman

---

Chugging along a country road in India in an outdated Ambassador which belonged to our hospital, I saw a little mother and two babes beside an Indian cot in a field. The day was cold. I wore my warmest coat.

Beside the mother was an old kerosene can filled with water from an irrigation canal close by. One child sat shivering on the bed. The tiny one was being soaped and splashed with water from the can.

Behind the trio was the hut they called home. Walls were covered with cow dung cakes drying in the sun. This was the family's only fuel for cooking and warming. The miniature mother was doing her best to keep her little ones clean. Soon, she would carry them to the fields where they would have their potty time.

The picture of that humble, loving mother of

the open field, has remained with me these many years.

"Oh, God, how can I ever complain again?"

# *Janaki*

She was the proud mother of two Rhodes Scholars and the wife of a man who was both an outstanding medical administrator and a surgeon of great reputation. Janaki and Santokh, her husband, were Sikhs. It was easier for me to relate to them, for they were a one-god people. Their scriptures read like our Psalms.

We were about to return to the U.S. from our tour of duty in the Christian Medical College in Ludhiana when Dr. Santokh took me aside and said, "Olivia, I want Mel here in our Post Graduate School of Medicine in Chandigarh. If you will only say the word, he will come. Here is the house I have prepared for you. We will make you happy."

"Santokh, I have never had that much influence over my husband." But he didn't believe me. A letter from the Chief Minister of the Punjab

18

voiced the same sentiment, "If Mrs. Casberg will agree, I'm sure you will serve as Head of the Postgraduate School of Medicine here." Were these two gentlemen telling me something about the woman's influence in India?

This was the more remarkable in Janaki's case, for Santokh was a macho man. He stood tall, with beard, turban and deep voice; he made the ladies look and listen.

Women *do* have much to say about family affairs and decisions -- much more than I had ever suspected. But they do it so quietly and inoffensively that it usually isn't resisted.

Janaki built and furnished a beautiful home in the capital of the Punjab, Chandigarh. They had a swimming pool and a bathroom with a sunken bathtub, much like the one I designed for the Director's bungalow in Ludhiana. Both mine and theirs were constructed with chipped marble at a time when there were no bathtubs to be found in the marketplace.

She was a queen in her house, with many servants around. I can still hear her as she walked about the house with her ring of keys jingling in her belt -- keys that locked food cabinets and closets with coveted articles. In the mornings she busied herself with orders for food from the bazaar and giving her cook menus for the meals of the day. Laundry was counted out on the floor before the dhobi (laundryman) was trusted with it. The sweeper was assigned his duties for the day with a couple of rooms to be mopped and dusted.

Santokh came for a lecture tour to the U.S. in the '60s, and because we have always felt the Indian woman as well as her husband should visit abroad, we helped arrange honararia for Santokh so that Janaki could accompany him.

For decades, scholarships and visiting professorships have been given the *men* of India. I have contended that a country cannot be modernized or re-educated in the areas of preventive medicine and sanitary engineering, nor can they learn to make their homes comfortable and attractively decorated, unless the *women* see how it's done. Even our privileged Janaki learned a great deal about interior decorating in her contacts, both in our Indian home and in her visit to the States.

The bathroom problem -- my pet feud with India -- could be solved if the women of India insisted. Fields and water supplies could be cleaned up, so that amoebic infections and other related diseases could be greatly reduced. I do not see *why* this great country of India cannot tackle this sanitary problem and solve it.

Other countries do.

# Muslim Women
## in Purdah at Umri

She pulled aside the dark curtains of the window in the horse tonga as it approached our bungalow. The sick girls of the harem were left in the Dr. Sahib's office at the hospital. The others were free to visit the Memsahib. Here, they could drop their veils and see how the American lady lived.

I gave them the usual tour of the house. They were impressed with two things. The senior wife stopped in the study where our college diplomas hung. "You are so well educated," she said, "and yet, you came to us. Why?" Their curiosity then focused on my clothing. "Do you mind, Memsahib, if we look under your dress?" Fortunately, I hadn't succumbed to the heat that day. I did have on panties. And, of course, my usual bra, which I never left off, no matter how hot or humid.

They wore neither garment. Petticoats and

tight blouses were quite enough under the layered sari.

"How in the world," I asked my husband later, "do these women unveil and undress for you?" He explained that there is something in their mores which allows it under the watchful eye of an older woman.

This was my introduction to the Muslim women in Central India.

# The
# Little Cave Dweller

We saw her in front of her cave on a steep hill in Yenan, the old capital of Communist China. "May we see your home?" we asked. She was delighted.

We climbed up a long line of steps carved out of the loess soil and entered the compound, all neatly swept and hung here and there, like Christmas decorations, with strings of drying gourds, peppers and onions. A cave adjacent was stashed with thousands of apples from orchards very carefully tilled on sandy hills and irrigated with water, hand-carried from wells far below.

The home consisted of three caves, side by side, with inside doorways connecting them. Each cave measured ten feet wide and twenty feet deep. We entered the kitchen cave with its earthen floor and wooden cupboards all carefully decorated in bright flowers. There we met mother and a second daughter, both busy with the morning chores, grinding wheat and washing a few bowls. Mother was crippled with arthritis. Perhaps the dampness of the cave caused it. There was a stove, however -- a very ingenious one. It was built like a big earthen box with holes in the top where the cooking was done. The smoke with its warmth was not lost up a chimney but ran through another box-like structure the width of the cave, called the kang. This bed allowed the family a toasty warm area for the night. It really worked! We tried it once. The little family of three were far warmer in their cave than we were in our modern hotel room.

How generous they were when we left. They loaded us with fresh apples.

Their love of sharing is a heart-warming experience.

# The

# Eskimo Mother

---

I visited her in her humble hut made of willows and moss-covered tundra slabs. Her babe had been taken from under her parkah next to her bare back and brought around under the fur garment to her breast. A seal oil lamp heated and lighted the dark room. Piles of fur skins were stacked in the background on the floor -- covers for the family at bedtime.

I marvel as I think of these primitive people at Barrow in the early 1900s, before the oil invasion, and how they survived the 50 and 60 below zero temperatures.

My father, an explorer and archeologist, had grubstaked into Barrow and carried on our little schooner enough lumber to build a one-room cabin with several thicknesses of wood and tar paper for insulation. Our heating and cooking was done with seal blubber and coal dust. When we could find driftwood along the shore, we used that.

Eskimo babes in those days wore no diapers. How those mothers kept them clean I will always wonder. I remember in church they would take the little tikes out from under their parkahs and set them between their legs on a tin can, give a little stimulation with their hands and take care of the tee-tee. There were no public toilets in Pt. Barrow then. Men used the snow drifts and women squatted.

We had no china or silver. We ate on aluminum dishes with aluminum knives and forks. We boiled our meats, but the Eskimo were satisfied with frozen fish and whale skin, dipping often into the seal oil and licking their fingers loudly. We had no fresh vegetables, so we made do with dried potatoes, dried corn, dried eggs and canned milk.

The Eskimo mother was the meat man. She carved up the seal and walrus when they were brought in from the sea. Mother was the tailor. She sewed all the family clothes -- even the boots and shoes. She made the thread to sew the garments from the sinews of the animals they killed.

Their morals were rigid. There was no wife-swapping in that country, and no divorces that I ever heard of. But I don't remember ever seeing an unhappy Eskimo mother. She worked continously to survive the hardships and the cold.

Perhaps that was her secret of happiness.

# "Lucky"
## Dr. Lakshmi Rao

Our Medical College Registrar and Professor of Bacteriology was educated in Canada and turned Christian at an early age. She was very western in much of her thinking. She had a good foundation in drama. So each year she trained a goodly number of our medical students to put on professional plays. It was remarkable what good actors they became. The plays of Agatha Christie were favorites. "Witness for the Prosecution" was performed about as well as anywhere in the world.

Lucky was an External Examiner. She traveled to other medical schools to examine students in her specialty. There is a custom in India to have professors other than those in one's own institution give examinations.

So we, too, were caught up in this program. Every few weeks we would have a group of visiting professors come to our college to test our students. It was my duty to entertain them for dinner. It wasn't a simple meal, for I had to prepare a vegetarian dinner as well as one with meat and rice.

At first, I tried to seat my guests, western style. But I soon found that my distinguished professors preferred to eat standing. When they finished eating, on the floor, under the table went the soiled dishes.

Lucky managed several trips to the States through the years. Indian currency was impossible to get out of the country, so into her bags went some Indian silks which I would buy to help her with her traveling money. If she got stuck in a certain part of the States, she didn't hesitate to write, "I'd love to come and visit you, but I have run out of funds." So, off would go some ticket money. We always had space in our home to guest our Indian friends.

Lucky spent one Fourth of July with us and we had the good fortune to be invited to an estate high on the mountains behind Santa Barbara, where we saw an unusual display of fireworks over the ocean. There, Lucky met our family. This is very meaningful to the Indian. They could teach us a great deal about family ties.

We put Lucky on the plane for India, with all her many packages hand-carried. She wore a lovely sari, and my Nieman Marcus rain cape which she had admired. Oh, yes, she had on my watch too. It will mean far more to her than it would to me.

One lesson I learned from the Luckies of India. I learned to *share*. If a friend needed a bra or a girdle, or gloves for a wedding, a bit of perfume or a pair of nylons -- we didn't think twice -- we shared.

Lucky taught me happiness in giving.

# The
# Medical Student
# In India

---

They came -- 25 of those giggling 17-year-olds. Brilliant girls they were, having been chosen by their families because they had promise of becoming doctors. Hindus, Sikhs, Muslims and Christians -- all seeking "to serve suffering humanity" as they often wrote in their applications for medical school.

Their dress usually indicated their religion. The Punjabi Sikh girl wore pantaloons, pulled in tight at the ankles and an overblouse almost to the knee, with slits up each side. Around the neck, with the ends hanging down the back, was the ubiquitous scarf. A mark of modesty, they said. And they were never without it.

The Hindu girl was there with her sari, always a lovely, graceful garment. Sometimes it was wrapped around once, sometimes twice, so as to reveal the hips. There was always the "tail" of the sari more elaborately decorated. It was used to cover the head or face, or just as a shawl about the shoulders. Only amateurs pinned the sari to the shoulder. So the tail was always slipping from the left shoulder and being pushed back again in a coquettish fashion, much as the American girl will toss a lock of hair from her face. It was an attention-getting thing. Her hair was seldom short and so the one braid down the back, or a bun rolled at the nape of the neck were the most common styles. A red dot on the forehead and several bangles pretty well completed the costume.

We had 25 boys accepted at the same time and though many friendships were begun, permanent relationships were not encouraged because parents still arranged marriages. We would see ads in the newspaper which read:

> "Wanted: educated, beautiful, homely (homeloving) vegetarian bride of good family for Aggarwal bachelor 20 yrs. Postal officer, salary Rs. 350-p.m., respectable M.P. family. Sub-caste, province no bar. Apply with full details."

A courier would report to Mommy and she had a great deal to say as to the choice of a daughter-in-law.

The medical college was not the place to practice my Hindustani. The students were eager to improve their English, so the Memsahib was a good target. The entire curriculum was taught in English, by the Indian Professor as well as the foreign staff.

Our little giggling girls of 17 left us five years later, cultured, well-trained doctors, ready to go in to Government clinics or into residencies in the various specialties. India would be poor indeed without her many women doctors.

# *The*

# *Chinese Grandmother*

---

The T'ien An Men Square is a place where few Americans have walked for some 30 years; but shortly after Nixon's trip in 1972, Dr. Mel and I were invited to visit the People's Republic of China -- just the two of us, alone.

When I crossed that covered bridge from the Hong Kong side to what we had called the land of the Bamboo Curtain, I didn't know what to expect -- and I was scared. My fears soon softened, however, when we were taken into their homes, fed and housed in their best hotels and given transportation in their best cars, with a driver and two interpreters, one for each of us. Officials met us at each stop and we were wined and dined in a fashion fit for royalty. The tours in and around Peking included the Great Wall, Ming Tombs, a large Commune, The Summer Palace, a great Art Center and the Forbidden City.

We had been told that everyone works, including mothers of small children. Was the family unit intact then? Yes. Grandparents didn't go into Senior Citizens' Homes, but because they were needed, they remained in the family home, taking care of the pre-schoolers and doing the housework, shopping, cooking and mothering still. In the T'ien An Men Square and city parks, on any sunny day, grandmother could be seen taking a small child for an afternoon walk or wheeling a babe in a cart.

No more bound feet. All women wore pants. Not realizing the universal use of pants, that first day I wore my suit skirt to the Great Wall. My companion and I had just come out of a ladies restroom when a grandmother, daughter and her small girl-child came up to me and before we could realize what was happening, the child stooped over and looked under my skirt. Grandmother and mother were terribly embarrassed. But a smile and nod of understanding from me put them at ease. That little girl hadn't seen skirts before.

Older women are special in China. If they are not needed in the home, they find something else to do to help their country. I visited a tiny factory where they took solid-state circuits from an electronic company -- tossed out because of some imperfection -- melted them down in great vats, skimmed off the silver and made about 30 silver ingots a month.

Another group of women with few home duties and no grandchildren started an incense factory. Before I left, they insisted on giving me a box of incense which I hand-carried all the way back to the States. I still use it on special occasions, remembering my industrious grandmothers in the Commune. Gathering junk to create "Treasures from Trash" and sweetening the air with incense -- even my air -- does help to make the world a pleasanter place.

A new insight came as I watched these grandmothers. They told us that Chairman Mao had inspired a selfless spirit.

It's a great achievement, no matter from what source one learns this lesson.

# "The
# Most Beautiful Woman
# In Nepal"

Nepal? What could I expect? Dr. Casberg had been called to spend ten days evaluating hospital care in this far away country, so recently opened up to the world.

Katmandu lay in a valley at the foot of Mt. Everest, the headquarters of the famous mountaineer, Sir Edmund Hillary. Greeting us as we landed in Nepal were dozens of palace-like structures surrounded by formal gardens. One of these was to be our home for ten days. A refrigerator! A bath tub! And a screened-in verandah that was so long we could take our morning jog on it.

"Why," I asked, "all this affluence?" It was then explained that these palaces once belonged to the Ranas who collectively ruled the country for a hundred years before the late king came to power.

One day an invitation came from the uncle of the King, Kaiser Shamsher. As we entered the hall of the palace, there were two huge elephant tusks arching over our heads. Stuffed tigers in the corners completed the museum effect. Kaiser Shamsher then segregated the men from the ladies and told us that they would be back soon. Would we just make ourselves comfortable.

The men ascended a long stairway to his library, and there he displayed "the largest pornographic library in the Orient." When the men returned, our tour continued outside where he showed us four large buildings, one for each season of the year. These he used for large banquets and entertainments for special guests. A private lake beyond marked Kaiser Shamsher's personal area to hunt ducks.

Inside again, we were all led up several flights of steps and down a long hallway where a curtain of French lace hung from ceiling to floor. This he formally pulled aside, and we were escorted into a room with a large table in the center. There she stood ... "the most beautiful woman in the Orient!" We were properly introduced. She bowed low. Without a word she stepped to the table, opened a box of precious chocolates and began offering them to her guests. The sweets meant a great deal to them, for they had been shipped to India and then carried over a switch-back mountain road for 90 miles. She was a lovely statue. Not a word was spoken, but she smiled.

Dr. Casberg was bold enough to ask Kaiser Shamsher if he would mind if a picture were taken of her Highness. He was flattered. The following story of her conquest was told later by one of the servants.

> "It was time to arrange a marriage for one of the Kaiser's sons. A courier was sent out and he returned with great stories about a beautiful lady. She was asked to come to have an interview with the father. He was so impressed that he was said to have remarked, ' she is far too beautiful to give to my son; I shall have her. ' And forthwith, he built a home for the mother of his children, took this lovely beauty for his new wife and sent the courier to find another wife for his son."

He has practically imprisoned the Beautiful Lady because he fears that she will be taken from him. She lives behind French lace, but it might as well have been iron bars.

What price Beauty!

# The
# Floating Mother

---

Hundreds of families fled Mainland China after the war and Hong Kong was bulging at the seams. We were returning from a tour of duty in India and as our plane approached the harbor, I became aware of hundreds of small live-in boats along the shores. On our daily tours I was able to examine just how these Chinese families were living. Children were cued up at faucets along the shore for their daily water supply. Toilets drained into the harbor beside the boats. Dishes were washed in the same water, and children bathed and brushed their teeth in it. Tin huts built with five-gallon cans housed another group of refugees on the hills around the harbors.

"Where do these people get their food and medical care?" I wondered. And then, I heard about a Center to help the refugee mothers. It is called the "Christian Family Service Center".

Some wonderful person had decided to do something about the terrible plight of these people and had established a headquarters where the women could come during the day. There they would work on arts and crafts which they do so well, or, if duties demand their presence with babes at home, they were allowed to take the work with them. They were paid by the job. The Center found places to sell the products.

I bought a supply of brocade boxes, glass cases, tiny Chinese dolls, note paper with appliqued figures, aprons and purses. I first sold them from my home in Long Beach.

Then, I became manager of a hospital Gift Shop, a much better marketplace. Later, our church women found another outlet in their circles. And now, catalogues advertise and sell by mail order these products made by the floating mothers at the Christian Family Service Center.

Hundreds of mothers have come and gone from the Center. Their children ate. Their families survived until permanent work could be found.

# Rose Sardar Khan

Rose was a master of English. She knew so
many words in our language which expressed
beauty, happiness and hope that she wrote and
spoke as a poet. You know, it's important when
one is learning a new language to learn the good
and happy words.

Rose was married to a professor of some note.
She and her husband, Sardar, were children of
Muslims who accepted Christianity early in the
century. Rose and Sardar used to take a walk on
our Indian compound, and often, on a Sunday
evening, knock on our door. Charles, our cook,
would bring tea and cookies, and we talked of
their past, of Indian history, of the faith of their
forefathers, and of their hope for their four
children who were having difficulty in a country
which favored those of the native faiths. Today,
most of their children have taken citizenship in

Canada.

Rose looked at my wrists one day, and being the good friend that she was, said, "Olivia, you must learn to wear bangles. Even two would be better than none at all." She explained that Indians would respect me more. It is like a wedding ring for many. It was further suggested that I wear a nose ring and a red dot on my forehead, but I couldn't quite bring myself to that. In a part of the world where men rarely see legs, and when our American and European women were coming out to India in mini skirts, Rose thought it appropriate for me to wear the Indian sari. I loved it anyway. The alternative was the Punjabi pantaloon with its tunic overblouse and ubiquitous scarf. "Why the scarf -- always the scarf?" I asked one day.

"It's a matter of modesty," Rose warned, "and don't ever let a man take it from you."

She thought it best for me to let my hair grow. "A white face is quite enough of a curiosity," she explained. In this way, Rose eased me into the Indian scene and made it much more pleasant to accept the new mores of the country which I would call my own for several years.

# Senna — Wife of Charles, Our Cook

I saw her first cranking my ice cream freezer. I had ordered banana ice cream for guests that night. We had many who came to our bungalow from all over the world to study our Medical School and Hospital in the Punjab. The President of Harvard had been in for tea. We were expecting Wells Hangen, his wife and their little dog; Wells was the correspondent who later was lost somewhere in Cambodia.

I was determined to have as few servants as possible. Could I get along without an ayah for my children? I could -- and I would. But when I tried to do my own food shopping in the Indian bazaar, I found that my white face and foreign clothes doubled our food bill. So I settled for a cook who could bargain. Charles felt he was too good to soil his hands on cleaning floors or doing dishes, so we had to employ a sweeper *and* a house boy.

There were times when our western appetites longed for the taste of ice cream. And since we couldn't buy what we felt was dependably pure in town, I would usually elect to boil my own buffalo milk and stir up a gallon of banana, chocolate or papaya ice cream. Then, I could trust Charles to keep his fingers out of the mixture and do the rest of the procedure. But this day, I looked out on the back verandah to see another person on the crank. Charles had graduated and brought his little wife, Senna, to do his twisting of the freezer. Very soon, he had trained her to do our breakfasts, too, and we didn't mind a bit -- for she was a better maker of chappatis and congee (the equivalent of tortillas and cooked wheat meal).

Tragedy stalked Senna. She had eight girls! That in itself was enough to disgrace her for life. Charles had warned her never to take those pills they gave out at the Clinic. "They only make girl babes, all the servants knew that."

One morning Charles came into the kitchen crying, "Oh, Memsahib, another girl."

"I know just what you should do now, Charles. You can go into our hospital tomorrow and get fixed. Your doctor will explain it all very carefully. It takes little time, and you don't have to fear impotency. I assure you it won't hurt your love life."

But, do you think Charles would do it? NO.

This pattern of life is repeated in the millions in India. It seems hopeless to try and cope with the population problem. So people like my little Senna go on having babies every year, toting her latest on her hip as she goes about her motherly chores. Senna had it better than most, even so. There was a proper house for the family and food to feed them. Charles' salary was better than that of the other servants. It was just that they had too many girls.

It was difficult training my jungly couple to keep clean. We provided special coats for them when they entered the kitchen. Keeping the nails very short and washing the hands with soap were two rigid rules enforced.

There was always the threat of amoebic infection and hepatitis, for the personal habits of the Indians were such that amoeba are carried under the fingernails. And entire households can be infected with one careless handling of water. Scarcely a week went by but what we would have one or more of our foreign faculty hospitalized with dysentery.

When we left India we helped Senna and Charles build their own little shack for all those girls and grandgirls. They are, no doubt, still populating the Christian community there in the slums of the city we once called home.

# The
# General's Wife

She was a grandmother. Three times her husband had tried to retire, but when the President of the United States calls your husband to be his private physician, what can you say?

I met her at one of those tiresome cocktail parties in Washington. She was bored. So bored that she had found a quiet corner for sipping her gin and tonic alone.

"I drink," she explained as I took a little stool beside her, "because I'm downright sick of all this."

She told me that at any time and on a moment's notice, she and her husband could be called from what they were doing to join the President and his lady in the White House -- even for a game of cards.

She longed for her grandmotherly duties, and life was fast slipping by. What price public office!

Three years as the wife of the Assistant
Secretary of Defense had been quite enough for
my lifetime. I suffered for my friend, the General's
Lady, and understood a little.

# The Missi-Sahib

The foreign maiden-lady doctor on our compound was housed in a place called Lal Khoti (Red
Cottage). There were several women from different countries there. They had separate
bedrooms and sitting rooms. Each had a servant or
two, and they ate in a common dining room.

Maiden ladies in India, no matter what na-
tionality, had problems, I soon found out.
Motivated with service to humanity, many were
well educated and completely dedicated. But they
had problems.

Loneliness in a foreign country is exaggerated
and unduly magnified. Frustration with inconve-
niences like uncomfortable beds, bad food,
amoeba-laden water and polluted fresh vegetables.
They had to learn a new language. Their servants
were often unreliable. There were no beauty
parlors. Dresses designed and sewn in the bazaar

by derzis (tailors) were generally out of style. But most of all -- there was no one to love just *you.*

Their selflessness was commendable. Their reward in heaven will probably be a great deal more than the memsahib who had a husband.

We saw them come and go. Some stayed, and we saw lovely beauties turn into forlorn maidens.

# Radhakrishnan's Daughter

Dr. Casberg was called to a Central Indian Medical College for a lecture and some advice in medical problems. He invited me to go along. We were to be entertained in the home of a prominent doctor who was then the Medical Director of Hyderabad.

The Lady of the house was the daughter of the late President of India -- a delightful person. She had raised a family, and her children were successful professional people. I noticed her home showed unusual decor for an Indian residence, and she confessed she had been the architect.

She was an orthodox Hindu. She told us stories about her gods at the breakfast table that day. Then she asked me if I would like to see her holy place. The fact that she wanted to share her most intimate and spiritual things with me, a Christian, touched my heart. She took me upstairs to a large room much like a master bedroom. There on her walls were pictured large forms. Without heads. She noticed my surprise, for she explained that the gods were far too holy for her to look on their faces.

She must have loved me, for when we left, she gave me two elephant tables which still grace our home and remind me of my day with the daughter of the President of India.

# Mrs. Li

We had just said "Goodbye" to an NBC TV team headed by Nancy Jarvis. They were flying home to the States from Yenan, China. It was 1972. Nixon had just visited China. There was really no other way to get out of that isolated city except to fly, but the snow storm was closing in fast and the Chinese planes were grounded. We were stuck in the Cave City, the name I gave to the old capital of Communist China.

Our room in what I called, "The Hall of the Mountain King" was icy. The wind whistled down the wide corridors of the hotel every time a door was opened. Mrs. Li, my Chinese interpreter, had planned a tour for us that day, but due to the weather she had decided against it. When she came to our room she asked very timidly, "Would you mind helping me with my English? I have so many tours with lectures to give to the tourists, and my English is very poor."

I was glad to help her, of course. I put on all the warm clothes I had brought along, wrapped up in the hotel blankets, put a hot water bottle to my feet and we sat and talked in English for hours.

Six years later when with the Dixie Mission group of World War II we visited Yenan again, Mrs. Li was at the airport. It is very difficult to show our gratitude to the Chinese who accompany us on these trips. No tips are accepted and when we bring gifts, they say, "No, it is our duty to serve you."

"But this time," I pleaded, "for old friendship's sake, I want to leave something for you." One day, I spread a few little American things on my bed and asked her to come to my room and choose what she would like. Just as we were about to leave the States, I had slipped into the corners of my suitcase some flower and vegetable seeds. On the bed were many more attractive and interesting articles for her children or for her, but she chose only the seeds I had brought. "As these grow", she said, "I will think of you. I will always remember you."

Mrs. Li is serving her country in a very selfless way. Her husband works in another city, and her children make their home with him. She didn't divorce him nor did she choose to be so separated, but she explained, "My Government needs English-speaking interpreters here. The time will come when they can train more interpreters. Then, I can leave and be with my family again."

That same spirit of sacrifice was exemplified in a Commune Hospital we visited. An Ob-Gyn doctor of special qualifications gave up her city practice to go to a small hospital in the country where she could train Barefoot Doctors and take care of "special" cases. It's akin to the missionary spirit so strongly emphasized by Christians. One finds this large sign in cities: "FORGET SELF. LIVE FOR OTHERS."

Concern for their country they learn early. And concern for their country ultimately means concern for neighbors and fellow workers. Albert Schweitzer once wrote to Dr. Tom Dooley -- two great men from two other worlds:

I know not what your destiny will be
but this I do know: those of you who
will find real happiness will be those
who will have sought and found
HOW TO SERVE.

Mrs. Li learned this lesson well. What an example for us!

# *Su Fei*

I just can't think of Su Fei without George.
These newlyweds joined Mao and his Chinese
followers in the mid 1930's as they finished the
"Long March" to freedom in the great western
wasteland which is now a part of The People's
Republic of China.

George, a new graduate of the University of
Geneva Medical School, and looking for a
challenge, joined the Communists. Their need for
medical care was the greatest he had seen in the
world. He married the lovely Shanghai actress, Su
Fei, took the name of Ma Hai-teh, and began a
career which in the last 25 years has done more
for more people than any doctor in history that I
know of.

Under his tutelage China has done a magnificent job of public health, practically wiping out
venereal disease, controlling drug addiction and

helping rid China of prostitution -- "except on borders where we can't control foreigners", as they say. Flies are few. All drinking water is boiled.

In spite of the greatness of her husband, Su Fei carried on her own professional career. She raised two children who are now active in the New China. In recent years she has contributed significantly to the production of movies China makes for their children. And our last information from her is that she will soon be involved in a documentary of a Chinese "Roots." A very fond grandmother, she finds time to bathe her little grandson at the close of a busy day. Her son and his wife live in a wing of her home. You see, sons bring their brides to live in the family house.

Sue Fei is a delightful hostess. In China it is the usual thing to entertain guests in a hotel dining room, but ours was a unique privilege to dine with the family in their Peking home, renewing a friendship which began during the years of World War II.

Two gifts we took them. One, a musical panda which played Brahm's Lullaby for the tiny grandson; the other, a story for children, "The Little White Girl in Eskimoland" (my life, written and illustrated by my explorer father).

Su Fei conformed to the rigid styles of the Chinese women with short hair, baggy pants and Chinese coat-blouse. But she has great personal freedom. No padding along behind her husband, head down and submissive.

She enjoys equality on all levels, perhaps even more than the average American woman.

Su Fei is princess-like.

She is a happy woman.

# Two Missionary
# Doctors Wives On
# Shipboard

It was the month of the greatest number of sinkings in the Atlantic. Guns of World War II blazed.

The east coast of India felt more and more the onslaught of invasion. Colombo was being bombed, and Americans were asked to leave. The steamship Brazil, which had brought out 5,000 troops to Bombay, was ordered to evacuate as many Americans as possible.

Nancy and her two little ones had been left alone in Iran. The American Army had ordered her husband to join forces in the C.B.I. (China, Burma, India). Everything except their clothes was to be left behind. They escaped by taxi, horse tonga and train -- just anyway she could find, in order to arrive at the evacuation port in time.

Our family, including elderly Father and Mother Casberg, and our two small children, met the group of 1,500 evacuees from all over Southeast Asia at the port of Bombay. Our sailing date was uncertain, so we waited some time before we were allowed on ship.

We came all the way in blackout, with rationed water and standing-room-only at meals except for those who had small children. Husbands and wives were assigned to different parts of the ship. Mothers with children were housed in what was once the Officer's Quarters, with beds stacked only three tiers high. The men slept in the bowels of the ship with four or five layers of bunks.

Father Casberg had only one leg, so he was quite dependent on his son to help him get to meals and the frequent life boat drills. Nancy and I with our four children were given a room near the life boats.

The officers on shipboard were a nervous bunch of men, for we had two hundred children aboard. I heard one of them say one day, "We will NEVER be able to get these kids overboard if anything happens!"

And, as if things weren't confused enough, someone came on ship with two virile bugs, and in a short time we had a hundred cases of whooping cough and measles, and some of the children had both. The fifteen doctors on board were kept busy.

Subs and surface raiders forced the ship to zig-zag constantly (five minutes one way and five minutes the other). We had no hot water. The blackout became unnerving at times, especially when we were caring for the sick ones. Nancy and I struck up a most unusual friendship with our four sick children in one cabin, all under six years. Three single ladies had also been assigned to our noisy stateroom, but we didn't see much of them. Even at bedtime we wondered where they kept themselves.

The Brazil was finally dubbed the Ghost Ship because several radio messages went out that we had been sunk. We touched only one port. There we picked up survivors of 12 sunken ships. These boys were nervous, too. They wouldn't take off their clothes, and one would rarely see them without their life jackets. There weren't enough life boats for the passengers, so many men were assigned to rafts. The survivors we picked up spent most of their time in the shadows of those rubber rings.

One of the surgeons aboard, a man of 76 years, spiked a hot appendix, and since the ship's doctor was drunk most of the time, one of our passengers put a surgical staff together and did the surgery. It was interesting to hear the doctors describe how they would reach for an instrument and it would go sliding away from them, because of the tip of the ship as it turned to zig or zag.

Sundown and dawn were the times of greatest danger. To keep up morale, some of us organized choirs and orchestras. Nancy was expert on the violin and joined the orchestra. I formed a High School three-part girl's chorus. We had only four books which I had slipped into the suitcase as we left India, so the girls had to memorize their music. They were wonderful. And in the sunset hours on deck, as the crowds of nervous people gathered, the girls did a magnificent job of raising morale.

My other group was a four-part adult choir. They functioned at special worship gatherings. What a wonderful lift they gave the passengers as they reinforced morale with

Under His wings, I am safely abiding,
Though the night deepens and tempests are wild.

Or,

> Day is dying in the west,
> Heaven is touching earth with rest.
> Holy, holy, holy, Lord God of Hosts
> Heaven and earth are full of Thee,
> Heaven and earth are praising Thee
> Oh, Lord most high.

Always closing the hour with,

> Now the day is over.
> Through the long night watches
> May Thine angels spread their white
>     wings above me,
> Watching round my bed.

Our guardian angels brought us safely into Bermuda Harbor. The ship just ahead of us had gone down with 300 aboard; so it was decided to keep us in port for several days before proceeding home. This last run, we were told, was the most dangerous of all.

No one was allowed on shore. As night came on we watched the search lights span the skies for enemy planes. Three days in harbor, and we were on our way again with an airplane circling about on the edge of the horizon. A destroyer, like a mother hen protecting her chicks, swept away the enemy ahead. A submarine must have come close at one point, for depth charges were put off shaking up the ship like an earthquake.

Nancy and other mothers without their husbands were exceptionally calm in spite of sickness and the need to get their babes at any given signal into life belts and onto life boats.

One night after leaving Bermuda, Nancy and I stayed on deck as long as we could keep awake. But when the children got restless, we said "Goodnight" and proceeded down the long, dark stairways to tuck in our little ones on the two bunks above us.

Nancy said, "Let's not undress. We can put our purses and hats close by." We had been warned never to leave the ship without hats. We laid down on the floor beside the lower bunk. I fell into an uneasy sleep, and then awakened with a start.

The ship's engines had stopped and we were drifting. I had left my stateroom door ajar. I was aware of a clicking sound coming from the hall. There, in the dim blue light of blackout, I saw a figure passing by. It was the night watchman with his stopwatch. I knew I wasn't supposed to ask questions, but I ventured a little one, "Why have our engines stopped?"

"Lady ... we are in the channel of New York!"

Nancy and I bounced out of the room and up to the deck -- skipping steps all the way. There, along the horizon, ONE SOLITARY LIGHT pierced the darkness we had known for six long weeks. We knew we were safe. Soon, dawn broke and the people gathered.

It was a misty morning in New York. Through the fog, I caught a glimpse of the Lady of Liberty. There she was -- standing with head and torch high above the fog covering her base. She looked like an angel.

A Flying Tiger, who had escaped in disguise as a priest in a row boat and had swum ashore at Colombo through a barage of bombs, stood behind me. He was talking to the Statue of Liberty. "If you ever see me again," he said aloud, "you will have to turn around." Oriental topees, the last vestige of the Far East, were thrown overboard. Someone struck up the refrain, "God Bless America" and EVERYONE cried.

My dear Nancy, with her two children, have no Daddy now. He lost his life. But with astounding courage, she wrote to me,

> Forgetting those things which are behind, and reaching forth unto those things which are before -- I press forward.

GOD BLESS AMERICA.